Christmas 2002
David Ford

PRACTICAL FISHKEEPING

FEEDING AQUARIUM FISHES

Dr. David Ford

Dr. David Ford

RINGPRESS

ABOUT THE AUTHOR

Dr David Ford CChem, FRSC, MPhil, PhD, has been a keen aquarist for more than 50 years. He is a chartered chemist with higher degrees in the physical chemistry of aqueous systems, plus a food science degree, and so was chosen to develop the Aquarian® range of fish foods in the 1970s. David then started the Aquarian® Advisory Service, which he has been running ever since. He has dealt with more than 100,000 fishkeeping problems, lectured to more than 300 aquarist clubs, and written numerous articles and books, which have been published worldwide.

SCIENTIFIC CONSULTANT: Dr. Peter Burgess BSc, MSc, MPhil, PhD is an experienced aquarium hobbyist and international consultant on ornamental fish.

Commercial products shown in this book are for illustrative purposes only and are not necessarily endorsed by the author.

Photography: Dr. David Ford (p.8, p.35, p.45, p.57, p.60),
Keith Allison, and courtesy of Tetra U.K.
Line drawings: Viv Rainsbury
Picture editor: Claire Horton-Bussey
Design: Rob Benson

Published by Ringpress Books,
a division of Interpet Publishing,
Vincent Lane, Dorking, Surrey, RH4 3YX, UK
Tel: 01306 873822   Fax: 01306 876712
email: sales@interpet.co.uk

First published 2002
© 2002 Ringpress Books. All rights reserved

ISBN 1 86054 255 7

Printed and bound in Hong Kong through
Printworks International Ltd.

10 9 8 7 6 5 4 3 2 1

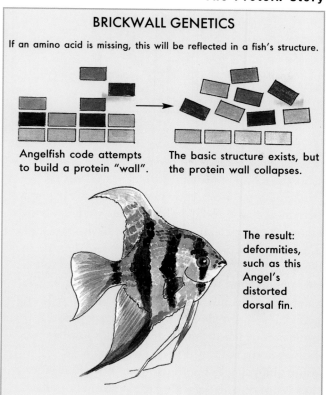

BRICKWALL GENETICS

If an amino acid is missing, this will be reflected in a fish's structure.

Angelfish code attempts to build a protein "wall".

The basic structure exists, but the protein wall collapses.

The result: deformities, such as this Angel's distorted dorsal fin.

protein diets designed for fish farming to pet fish. A balanced diet is the ideal diet and that means levels of digestible protein that will give good growth and maintenance, leaving carbohydrates to supply the energy.

Look for values around 34 per cent digestible protein for goldfish, 37 per cent digestible protein for tropical fish and 38 per cent digestible protein for marine fish.

CHAPTER 3

LIPIDS: FATS AND OILS

In the early 1800s, a German chemistry teacher, Justus von Liebig, established the very first experimental laboratories for students. With these students he studied extracts from body tissues and was the first to determine that carbohydrates and fats were the body's source of energy. Liebig used a glass device now called a 'Liebig condensor' to digest tissues and separate their components. He discovered the body fats and called them lipids from the Greek word 'lipos', meaning 'fat'.

However, because of Liebig's methods of 'refluxing' everything (i.e. boiling a liquid in a flask with a condenser attached so the vapour is not lost by evaporation), lipids was the name given to all compounds that did not dissolve in water but did dissolve in organic solvents such as alcohol or ether. Hence the term covers many compounds that we now know include fats, oils, waxes, fatty acids etc.

FATTY ACIDS

Each chemical group is amazing in its complexity and fascinating in the way nature has used their properties. There are two major groups of lipids important to fish: fats and oils. Chemically they are the same, being composed of carbon, hydrogen and oxygen, just like the carbohydrates. Certain lipids exist in life as mildly acidic forms, called 'fatty acids'.

Essential fatty acids must be present in a fish's diet.

Some fatty acids are made by man, or fish, in the actual digestive processes, but some have to be ingested in their correct chemical form. These are called the 'essential fatty acids' and must be present in any diet for it to constitute 'complete nutrition'.

CARBON: LIFE CHEMICAL

Carbon chemistry is fundamental to life. Carbon has four valencies (arms to which one, two, three or four other atoms can attach – called bonding). If all four arms are bonded completely and separately, the carbon is said to be 'saturated',

Carbon has four valencies (arms) to which other atoms can bond.

but if double or even treble bonds are present, the carbon is said to be 'unsaturated'. This is where the names 'saturated fats' and 'unsaturated fats' originate – see any advertisement for margarine.

SATURATED

One basic difference in carbon chemistry is that, when saturated, the compound has a higher melting point. This is because a carbon atom with all four valencies bonded – the arms outstretched – has a crystalline structure and can pack together to give a solid form (the ultimate is the diamond).

UNSATURATED

Unsaturated carbon compounds have less rigid structures; the double (e.g. C=C) and treble (e.g. C≡C) bonds give a kink in their molecular shape and so cannot pack together so well. This gives a liquid that only solidifies at very low temperatures. At normal temperatures, the so-called hard fats (butter, lard) are solid and are mainly composed of saturated carbon; unsaturated fats are liquid (cod-liver oil, cooking oils).

STORED ENERGY

Nature exploits this solid-liquid behaviour in fat storage. In humans (and other warm-blooded animals) fat is stored in adipose tissue (under the skin), and gives us our curves and body shapes. Since, in warm-blooded animals, this tissue is about 37°C (or 98.4°F), a liquid oil would be a problem – resulting in us losing our body shape entirely. However, at that temperature, hard fats are a soft solid, ideal for movement, protection and body shape.

If fish stored the same kind of fats, they would be as hard as a candle because even tropical fishes are more than 10°C (or some 25°F difference) cooler than their owners. Hence fish store fats as oils made from unsaturated carbon compounds, which remain liquid even at 0°C (which is important to cod swimming in Icelandic waters!).

The cold-blooded fish must store fats as oils.

FAT STORAGE

SATURATED
(e.g. lard)

$-\overset{|}{\underset{|}{C}}-\overset{|}{\underset{|}{C}}-\overset{|}{\underset{|}{C}}-$

UNSATURATED
(e.g. oil)

$-\overset{|}{C}=\overset{|}{\underset{|}{C}}-$

	% OIL IN	
	flesh	liver
COD	0.4	70
HADDOCK	0.3	70
HERRING	11	2
MACKEREL	13	8
SARDINE	13	NIL

TADPOLE CHEMISTRY

The main chemical structure of these fats is a molecule shaped like a tadpole, with a head of methyl (CH) groups that are oily and non-water soluble. The tail is an acidic group (carboxyl group COOH) that is water-soluble. This means the fish can dissolve the acidic end of the 'tadpole' in its bloodstream and so carry the oily end to a storage site (e.g. the liver or muscles).

Although called 'fatty acids', the tails are not actually acidic because they are neutralised by reacting with compounds such as glycerol to give so-called 'triglycerides' – a term often seen in nutrition. It is the unsaturated triglycerides that are stored in the muscles (the oily fish) or the liver (e.g. cod-liver oil) where it is held as a future energy source.

PHOSPHOLIPIDS

Another way of neutralising the acid tails is to react with phosphorus compounds to give phosphates (that is why the mineral phosphorus is needed in fish diets). These are called 'phospholipids' and can be found in all the membranes of the fish, making the compounds part of a fish's actual structure.

For the fish to be able to swim, the body needs to flex and bend even in the coldest waters; therefore

Phospholipids have a low-solidifying temperature, meaning a fish's body will stay flexible in tropical or cold waters. Pictured: Angelfish, *Pterophyllum scalare* (left), and Discus, *Symphysodon discus* and *Symphysodon aequifasciatus* (right).

unsaturation, or low-solidifying temperature, is important in phospholipid structure as well as triglyceride storage. Most fish need about 50 per cent phospholipids and 50 per cent fatty acid in their diet.

The phospholipids are held in the fish's body cells, but the fatty acids are stored as free globules and dissolved back into the bloodstream when needed. The carboxyl tails are oxidised by oxygen taken from the blood (dissolved from the water via the gills) in a reaction that releases energy.

In fact, the amount of energy released per gram of fat is twice the amount of energy obtained from carbohydrates (sugars). This is why it is more economical to store potential energy as fat (or oils) than as carbohydrates (unlike the vegetable kingdom which stores potential energy as pure carbohydrates – the sugars and starch).

THE OMEGA

The head of that fatty tadpole, or methyl end, is present as one of four main groups:

- Linolenic
- Linoleic (the spelling difference causes confusion!)
- Oleic
- Palmitoleic.

The bulk of fish oils are linoleic type, meaning it has a solidifying temperature of minus 5°C when in the structure of C18:3, Omega3. The following explains what this means.

CHEMICAL NAMES

There are no less than 35 rules that decide what name is given to an organic chemical. The four fatty acids found in fishes are:

- CH_3-CH_2-CH $\quad$ = $\quad$ the linolenic type
- CH_3-$(CH_2)_4$-CH = $\quad$ the linoleic type (the most common one)
- CH_3-$(CH_2)_7$-CH = $\quad$ the oleic type
- CH_3-$(CH_2)_5$-CH = $\quad$ the palmitoleic type.

The total number of carbon atoms is the C number. The number after the colon is the total number of double bonds (i.e. the amount of unsaturation). There are three in linoleic, since it consists of three chains (see structure shown above) i.e. 18 carbons.

But where are the double bonds? Counting the carbon groups (rather than individual atoms) from the first one to where the double bond occurs reveals this and it is given the Greek symbol 'omega': w In the

Feeding Aquarium Fishes

common linoleic, this is Omega3 (or *w*3) i.e. three
carbon groups along the chain.

Look at food supplements for humans and you will
find Omega3 oils for sale 'for your heart'. Saturated fats
can clog arteries, but oils will not, so fish oils are better
for you, and the common one is C18:3, *w*3. It may, or
may not, prolong *your* life, but it is essential for the life
of a fish.

COLD VERSUS TROPICAL

There are even differences between the fatty acids of
coldwater and tropical fishes. Coldwater species have

Coldwater species, such as the Goldfish, *Carassius auratus* (above),
have a different fatty acid structure to tropical species, such as the
Guppy, *Poecilia reticulata* (below).

shorter chain lengths and more double bonds, obviously to give a more oily texture at lower temperatures. There is even a difference between tropical freshwater and tropical marine fishes – the latter have more $w6$ fats than freshwater fishes. It is not yet understood why, but obviously the difference needs to be taken into account when designing a recipe for coral fishes.

CONSEQUENCES

Do not feed the hard fats of our diet to your fish. The fish will try to store the fat in the liver where it will be visible as a hard lump rather than the fluid globule it should be. The fats could also be converted to phospholipids with structural complications for the fish, especially coldwater species.

The following foods should be on the forbidden list:
• Burgers
• Hams
• Sausages
• All other red meats, especially fatty ones
• Many boxed convenience foods (e.g. microwave dinners and 'ready' meals).

Any food scraps that are given to your fish must be Omega-rich such as fish meat, shellfish, or at least low-fat foods such as white meat.

It is always obvious on a post-mortem examination of a fish if it has received a fatty diet: the liver will be swollen and pale, sometimes with spots of hard fat. The fish will never have been a good specimen in its shortened life.

CHAPTER 4

CARBOHYDRATES

Herbivores (plant-eaters) and omnivores (plant- and meat-eaters) can digest carbohydrates and use them as a source of energy. Practically all ornamental fish are omnivores. The complex carbohydrate (CHO) chemicals (page 25) are reduced to glucose by enzymes and taken around the body in the blood for instant use as energy – in just the same way we humans do. There is one great advantage in using carbohydrates for energy (rather than protein as discussed in Chapter Two), namely the end products are simply carbon dioxide, breathed out by the fish through the gills, and water.

Using carbohydrate as an energy source rather than protein results in less aquarium pollution. Pictured: Angelfish (*Pterophyllum scalare*).

Fish require less energy than most other animals. Pictured: South American Ram Cichlid (*Mikrogeophagus ramirezi*).

CHEMISTRY OF CARBOHYDRATES

For those familiar with chemical symbols, these are the reactions when fish need energy:

Carbohydrate CHO + digestive enzymes = $C_6H_{12}O_6$ glucose

Glucose + $6O_2$ (oxygen in the blood) = $6CO_2 + 6H_2O$ + energy (actually 673 kcals)

This is the same reaction that occurs in humans, but less efficiently. In fact, nutritional researchers have compared a fish's insulin control to that of a diabetic.

ENERGY NEEDS

The amount of energy fish need is much lower than most other animals. This is because fish are cold-blooded, so the large amount of energy spent by more highly evolved animals in maintaining warm blood is not needed.

Animal	Daily Energy Requirement (kJ* per kg body weight)	
Budgerigar	1,670	*a kJ is the scientific method of counting 'calories' – it is in kilojoules, and, if divided by 4.2, will give the equivalent amount in the older term of kilocalories, popularly known as just 'Calories' (note that 1 Calorie = 1,000 calories).
Dog	460	
Human	190	
Goldfish	40	

The support of the water means less energy is needed for moving around (land animals have to fight gravity all the time). Even breeding is less energetic – higher animals succour their young, most fishes just scatter eggs and ignore (or even eat) the results.

On the other hand, some species of fish (such as a Guppy or Platy escaping the attentions of a large Angelfish) have some of the fastest reaction times in all the animal kingdom. This swift flight from danger demands sudden bursts of energy.

The Guppy, *Poecilia reticulata*, has one of the fastest reaction times of any living creature.

ENERGY UTILIZATION

Research into energy utilization involves three different levels: gross energy (GE), digestible energy (DE) and metabolisable energy (ME).

GROSS ENERGY

This is the gross energy and shows the potential energy of a given food by burning it completely in pure oxygen and measuring the heat given off (the machine that does this is called a 'calorimeter'). No animal can use all this GE since it may not be able to digest it totally, or oxidize it so efficiently.

DIGESTIBLE ENERGY

The amount that is digested and absorbed is DE, the digestible energy. It can be measured by finding the energy in the faeces, by burning in oxygen then subtracting this from the GE.

Energy from a plant source is more digestible to herbivore and omnivore species (such as the Goldfish, *Carassius auratus*, above) than to carnivore species (such as the Piranha, left).

METABOLISABLE ENERGY

However, not all that energy is absorbed, some being lost via urine and across the gills (branchial excretion) so the third energy type is ME, metabolisable energy. The DE and ME content of foods depend upon their composition and the species that eat them. For example, the energy from a plant source is more digestible to the Goldfish than to a Piranha.

The results of energy level assessments by the WALTHAM®Aquacentre are shown below:

Species and Initial Size in Grams	Energy		Feeding	
	DE/fish /day	Joules	Mg/fish /day	Flakes /day
Goldfish *Carassius auratus*	3.6	239	14.4	2.4
Neon Tetra *Paracheirodon innesi*	0.18	68	3.8	0.6
Zebra Danio *Danio rerio*	0.3	128	7.2	1.2
Kribensis *Pelvicachromis pulcher*	1.0	182	10.2	1.7
Moonlight Gourami *Trichogaster microlepis*	1.9	508	28.5	4.9

(Flake diet based on AQUARIAN® at a DE of 1665kJ/100g (goldfish flakes) and 1783kJ/100g (tropical flakes). Goldfish were maintained at 20°C/68°F and tropicals at 26°C/79°F.)

MAINTENANCE ENERGY

At a given water temperature, the amount of energy a fish requires depends on how fast it is growing, as well as its swimming activity, but the minimum energy it needs to survive is called the maintenance energy.

The maintenance energy of fishes is less than 10 per cent of the value for mammals and birds. This is because fish are ectothermic (cold-blooded), whereas mammals and birds have to spend considerable energy maintaining their warm body temperature.

SPECIES NEEDS

It will be seen that to maintain a small tropical fish takes very little food – just over half a flake per day for a Zebra Danio, even a large Gourami can exist on less than five flakes a day (providing it is a good-quality, balanced diet fish food, of course, with a flake size of 10 to 15 mm or $^1/_3$-$^1/_2$ inch).

The metabolisable energy requirement of Koi, *Cyprinus carpio*, kept outdoors will vary according to the water temperature.

The ME required by goldfish is very different to tropicals kept at a constant temperature. Being ectothermic, their body temperature will rise with water temperature and this, in turn, leads to higher ME. Studies have shown that the maintenance food requirement of goldfish increases nearly three-fold as water temperature rises from 20°C to 24°C (68°-75°F).

For Koi kept in garden ponds, the ME requirement will double as the water rises from 10°C to 20°C (50°-68°F). Conversely, at 5°C (41°F), the energy requirement of pond fish is very low and feeding stops. Below 5°C (41°F), digestion and absorption is so slow that the fish enters a quiescent state and energy reserves are used until the spring brings rising temperatures. This is why, unlike aquarium fish, pond fish need a high level of digestible energy food in late summer and autumn.

DIGESTIBILITY

No dietary requirement for carbohydrates has been demonstrated in fish. This is simply because they can utilise protein as an energy source and that exploits the protein-rich live foods eaten by most species in the wild. As stated, this leads to ammonia excretion, subsequent high nitrite levels, and problems with nitrates in the closed water systems of aquaria. If the fish is fed a diet that requires it to utilise carbohydrates as an energy source, the fish must be able to digest these particular nutrients. For example, herbivorous fish have long, coiled intestines to promote microbiological digestion of carbohydrates.

The Common Goldfish, for example, does not have a stomach and yet has been called 'the underwater cow' because of its ruminant-like digestive system. The

The intestines of a Platy (*Xiphophorus maculatus*) are longer than the body, so the fish spends most of its day feeding on algae.

Guppy and Platy have intestines that are much longer than their bodies, which they fill with vegetable matter by browsing on algae-coated surfaces all day long.

Carnivores have short intestines but true stomachs, the latter designed to hold prey and digest the meal by enzymic solution rather than intestinal micro-flora. Some species will even regurgitate the remains of a meal rather than pass everything through to the anus. The most famous example is the Red-tailed Catfish, which can expel a half-digested meal with devastating consequences for the fish if housed in an ordinary-sized aquarium.

Many studies have been made on Trout and they have been shown to utilise only 25 per cent of carbohydrates in the diet, whereas carp can utilise twice this amount. Other studies have shown that the digestibility of carbohydrates is temperature-dependent. Carp will certainly digest more carbohydrates as the water temperature rises.

There are also indications that tropical freshwater fish can digest more carbohydrates than tropical marine fishes. This is one of the reasons why marine fish food is slightly higher in protein content (and hence lower in carbohydrates) than tropical freshwater fish foods.

Overfeeding does not cause obesity in fish, but can result in health problems. Pictured: healthy Two-spot Barbs (*Barbus ticto*).

CONSEQUENCES

Once upon a time, commercial fish foods were nothing more than biscuit crumbs. It is a monument to a fish's powers of survival that they managed to live on such a pure carbohydrate diet. Nowadays, commercial foods are protein-rich and contain balanced levels of carbohydrates from vegetable and cereal sources, chosen for their high digestibility.

Biscuit, bread, cake and similar carbohydrate-based foods are just not suitable for fish. Choosing brown bread rather than white, as some recommend, is not the best advice!

Fish do not become obese in the human sense because they have the ability to eat continuously, digest what they need, and excrete the rest. However, overfeeding carbohydrate can lead to related disorders. The force-feeding, for rapid growth, of farmed edible fish gives a common condition called 'liver glycogenosis' (or fatty liver degeneration) in which the liver swells with fat.

Overfeeding raw or processed cereals will lead to pet fish suffering these problems too. One example is the fat-bellied Koi fed too much bread for many years, which could have been a large but sleek prize-winner if given a balanced diet.

CHAPTER 5

VITAMINS

It was an American chemist called Casimir Funk who isolated the first substance now called a vitamin, from brown rice. He discovered the compound to be an organic derivative of ammonia, called an amine, so he chose the name 'vitamine' from the term 'vitae', which is Latin for 'life'. He combined 'vitae' with the chemical name of amines when it was discovered that this particular group of chemicals was essential for life itself.

Later more 'vitamines' were discovered, such as the vitamin C from limes eaten by British sailors (hence the colloquial use of Limey) or the vitamin D in cod-liver oil, curing ricketts. When isolated, these chemicals were found not to be amines, so the 'e' was dropped from their original name to help clarify things.

As they were discovered, the vitamins were logically named vitamin A, B, C etc., but errors developed. Vitamin B was found to be a mixture, hence B_1, B_2, B_3 was needed. Then 3, 4 and 5 were found to be the same chemical, so the next correct one became B_6. Eventually, we had B_{12}, but not until after B_{10} and B_{11} were found not to be vitamins after all!

TRACE ELEMENTS

Nowadays, vitamins belong to the 'trace elements', a title used by nutritionists to mean the elements of food that are present in only minute amounts, but are

Trace elements are essential for health and growth.
Pictured: *Cyrtocara moorii*, (Dolphia cichlid).

essential for health and growth. These include minerals and phytochemicals (see Chapter Seven), as well as vitamins. It is no coincidence that the compounds are only present in trace amounts because their effect is so powerful that excess can be harmful, indeed life-threatening.

The current (i.e. from the latest research) level of vitamins necessary for maintaining a fish's normal physiological functions are in the chart (right):

FAT-SOLUBLE VITAMINS

Vitamins can be grouped into water-soluble and fat-soluble

The minimum nutritional levels required by fish	
A	10,000 IU
D	2,400 IU
E	100 mg
K	10 mg
B1 (thiamine)	10 mg
B2 (riboflavine)	10 mg
Niacin	50 mg
B6 (pyridoxine)	10 mg
B12	0.02 mg
Pantothenic acid	50 mg
Folate	10 mg
Inositol	440 mg
Choline	2,000 mg
Biotin	1 mg
C	250 mg

Values per kilogram of dry diet (WALTHAM® Aquacentre 1999). No single foodstuff contains all these vitamins in the correct levels, emphasizing the need for a mixed (but balanced) diet.

types. The fat-soluble ones – A, D, E and K – are absorbed into the fish's stored fats (oils). This means they can build-up to toxic levels if too much is supplied. Known as hypervitaminosis, a particular problem for fish is vitamin A, which can be supplied in excess if too much fish oil is included in the diet.

A classic example of the danger of Vitamin A is that polar explorers are warned not to eat polar bear meat, because their diet of polar fish is so rich in the vitamin that just one meal could kill the human! The fish themselves tolerate the chemical, but, if given in excess, it will give 'hypervitaminosis A', which causes slow growth, anaemia, and fin rot.

LEACHING

One problem is that water-soluble vitamins leach into the aquarium (or pond) water when flake, granules or pelleted foods are added.

This can be quite a significant loss: for example, up to 90 per cent of vitamin B_{12} content of a flake can be lost within 30 seconds (below). To overcome this

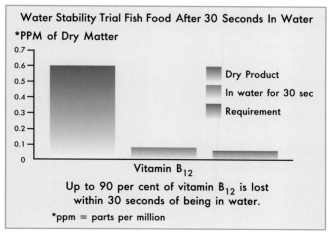

Water Stability Trial Fish Food After 30 Seconds In Water
***PPM of Dry Matter**

Dry Product

In water for 30 sec

Requirement

Vitamin B_{12}

Up to 90 per cent of vitamin B_{12} is lost within 30 seconds of being in water.

*ppm = parts per million

Bottom-feeders, such as the Corydoras Catfish, are the greatest victims of leaching, and require a flake food that contains insoluble forms of vitamins.

problem, insoluble versions of the vitamins are used. Alternatively, the mix is 'fixed' by blending with raw proteins that bind the vitamins as the protein is heated in the drying process.

Once the vitamin is dissolved into the water, it is lost to the fish but becomes a source of food for bacteria and algae, so adding to aquarium pollution. The fish most affected are the bottom-feeders and nutritional trials have shown that *Corydoras* Catfish actually lose weight when fed a standard flake diet. The fish only recovered when the vitamin mix was made non-water-soluble, i.e. only available to the fish on digestion.

The other trace elements, minerals, can also leach into the water, but, unlike vitamins, they are still available to the fish since certain elements can be absorbed back through the gills, fins and mouth, especially in marine species (because they drink some seawater).

DEFICIENCY PROBLEMS

The symptoms of vitamin deficiency are well known in many species of fish. Here are the most common effects:

Vitamin	Deficiency Symptom
Vitamin B_1 (Thiamine)	Poor appetite, nervousness, convulsions
Vitamin B_2 (Riboflavin)	Cloudy eyes, no growth
Vitamin B_6 (Pyridoxine)	Nervous behaviour, slow growth
Vitamin B_{12} (Cobalamine)	Slow growth
Biotin	Affects mucous layer; called 'blue slime disease'
Choline	Slowed growth
Folic acid	Slowed growth, blood spots in the kidney
Inositol	Poor growth
Niacin	Increased skin sensitivity (e.g. in ponds)
Pantothenic acid	Sluggish behaviour and 'blue slime disease'

CONSEQUENCES

Vitamin deficiency will give symptoms that resemble bacterial diseases or parasite infestation problems. The aquarist who feeds his/her fish with any diet that does not contain the correct level of a particular vitamin will see the described symptoms and assume an infectious disease is present.

Treatment is then given with chemicals such as Methylene Blue, Malachite Green, Acriflavine, or even worse, antibiotics (which may kill off valuable filter bacteria). These chemicals just add to the distress of the fish and cause a downward spiral that can lead to death.

Feeding good-quality foods prevents many health problems in the aquarium.

Other aquarists prepare their own foods and, recognising that fish need a range of vitamins, grind up multivitamin tablets or add liquid vitamin solutions. There are two problems with this do-it-yourself dieting: the fish need different levels of each vitamin than humans (and more of them too), and hypervitaminosis can result.

Cod-liver oil is often used by fishkeepers as a binding agent for food mixes, and is very rich in vitamin A; if this is also added in the multivitamin mix, the overdosing can give a symptom such as fin rot, as described above. The aquarist will certainly turn to classic fin rot remedies (which are antimicrobial) and never suspect that the basic cause was their home-made fish food.

The solution to the problem of water-soluble vitamins leaching is obvious: never buy cheap fish foods. Treatment of the original recipes to bind the vitamins into a form that is only released during digestion is complex and expensive, and this is reflected in the selling price.

CHAPTER

6

MINERALS

Fish have an 'open system' in that they interact across their skin/body surface with their environment. Humans live in a 'closed system' because we have a waterproof skin and only react with the outside world via gases in the lungs.

Life started in the oceans 600 million years ago, but by then the earth was already 4,000 million years old and those oceans were full of minerals, which were incorporated into the cells of the life-forms that eventually developed into the fishes.

A fish's mineral needs are as a result of its 'open system' which gives a direct interaction with its environment.

It is fascinating that the body fluids of modern fishes have the same salts as that primordial ocean, roughly 1 per cent solutions of sodium chloride, magnesium sulphate, calcium sulphate, and so on.

The oceans continued to concentrate the minerals from the land, via evaporation and rainfall, until the modern ocean is around 3 per cent salts. This causes all kind of problems to marine fish who have to cope with 'osmotic pressures' of the surrounding saltier seas, and also affects freshwater species that migrated from the seas with that 1 per cent salt content. However, that is a physiological topic, not a nutritional one.

ESSENTIAL MINERALS

The nutritional consequences of life developing in that primordial ocean are that certain minerals are now essential for body chemistry. The value of the minerals is shown in the following table:

MINERALS	REQUIREMENTS (per kg/2.2lbs dry diet)	VALUE TO FISHES
Calcium	5 g	99% is present in the bones
Phosphorus	7 g	80% is in the bones, the remainder in the cells where it is used for transferring energy
Magnesium	500 mg	Also used in the bones but also in metabolism of carbohydrates

Sulphur	3 to 5 g	Present in intracellular fluids and in several amino acids
Iron	50 to 100 mg	Essential for haemoglobin
Chromium	Trace	Only tiny amounts needed, but essential for growth
Manganese	20 to 50 mg	Activates several enzymes. Manganese-deficient fish can develop cataracts or bent spine (the latter in young fish)
Zinc	30 to 100 mg	Although deadly poisonous in the water, traces are still needed in the diet for efficient digestion
Copper	1 to 4 g	Another toxic chemical in the water if in excess, but without this metal, fish show poor weight gains

Feeding Aquarium Fishes

Selenium	Trace	Trials show the addition of selenium improves breeding condition, possibly acting with vitamin E
Iodine	Trace	Absence will give thyroid problems, just like it does with humans.

Quantitative measurements of the fishes' mineral needs is difficult because several of the chemicals can be absorbed from the water and so it does not matter if they are absent from the diet. Calcium, magnesium and sodium, for example, are present in all waters and are readily adsorbed by the fish when needed.

Fish can absorb several minerals, including calcium, magnesium, and sodium, directly from the water. Pictured: Garfish (*Ctenolucius hujeta*).

MINERAL DEFICIENCIES

Mineral deficiency is rare in wild and farmed fishes, since many compounds can be found dissolved in the water. Their effects have been studied anyway, under the following groups.

- **Structural:** these are used for teeth and bones and include calcium, phosphorus, fluorine and magnesium.
- **Respiratory:** haemoglobin in the blood containing iron, copper and cobalt.
- **Metabolic:** sodium, potassium, iodine and chlorine.
- **Trace elements:** boron, aluminium, selenium etc.

EFFECTS OF DEFICIENCY

Low structural chemicals (see above) will give poor bone structure; a classic example is 'bent spine' (the distorted spine in fishes is usually due to disease, such as fish tuberculosis).

If respiratory minerals are deficient, the fish will gasp at the surface as the oxygen level in the blood falls below critical levels. Such behaviour could be blamed on gill parasites or the oxygen levels in the water itself and aeration increased – with no effect on the symptoms.

Mineral deficiency can result in spinal deformity. Pictured: spinal deficiency in a Tetra.

A tumour on the tail base caused by an iodine deficiency.

Metabolic deficiencies are rare because most waters contain sodium and potassium. Chlorine is always present in water; indeed, it is present in excess in tapwaters and needs reducing anyway. Iodine deficiency gives goitre-like symptoms (i.e. a lump or a localised swelling), just the same as in humans.

WATER SOFTENERS

One problem with sodium is that it can occur in excess rather than a deficiency, giving metabolic problems for ornamental fishes. Water treated in the home to make it 'soft' for washing has calcium ions replaced by sodium ions, making it totally unsuitable for aquarium use. Any softening of water for pet fish needs ion removal, not exchange. Alternative water sources for soft-water-loving fish include: purification via distillation, reverse osmosis, or dilution with rainwater.

The trace elements are rarely absent in both diet and the water. Extra levels above naturally-occurring ones can have beneficial effects. For example, absence of selenium inhibits spawning behaviour and so fish farmers use foods with extra selenium for their breeding stock. Perhaps a selenium-rich fish food would help breeders of aquarium fish?

Commercial fish food is specially formulated to contain the correct quantity of minerals.

CONSEQUENCES

The common mineral elements are not needed in the fish's diet since they occur naturally in the waters of their natural environment – especially the coral fishes. But freshwater pet fish are almost always kept in tapwater which is purified beyond most natural waters. Imbalances in chemical content also occur in tapwater since coagulating chemicals are added to aid tapwater filtration, and pH adjustments are made with alkaline chemicals.

Unlike vitamins, an excess of any mineral is not a problem for fish, which can just digest whatever is needed, passing the residue through as faecal waste. This refers to trace levels, of course; a vast excess of any mineral will lead to toxicity.

Hence it is common practice to add a range of minerals to any fish diets at levels shown to be necessary from current knowledge. Control of those levels is beyond the ability of any aquarist who mixes their own diet – leave it to the experts!

CHAPTER
7

PHYTOCHEMICALS

Plants provide essential phytochemicals for fish.

Phytochemicals are the basic chemical structures of plants (derived from the Greek word 'phuton' meaning 'plant'). Animals (including fish) eat these plants and so utilise these phytochemicals – in turn the carnivores digest the same chemicals from the herbivores they eat. Hence the chemicals have become essential for life.

A classic example of a phytochemical is the compound in tomatoes that has been found to prevent certain cancers – health authorities are now recommending 'a tomato a day to keep the doctor away'. Perhaps this will also apply to fish – already carotenes (part of the red colour of tomatoes) are added to fish foods for their known benefits in research work.

COLOUR FOODS

Carotenoids are widely distributed in plants and more than 500 have been shown to create the colour of fruits

A combination of carotenoids and proteins produces the vivid colours seen in the Cardinal Tetra (*Cheirodon axelrodi*).

and vegetables (e.g. beta-carotene makes carrots orange).

Dietary carotenoids accumulate in a fish's skin in cells called chromatophores. Unlike plants, animals cannot synthesise these carotenoids, so they must be included in the diet. However, fish can convert one form of carotenoid to another, and this gives the variety of skin colours: e.g. goldfish can range from dark red to yellow.

Furthermore, fish can combine the carotenoid with proteins to give another range of colours called caroteno-proteins with purple and vivid blue colours, as seen in the popular Cardinal Tetra (*Cheirodon axelrodi*).

Additives to commercial diets to supply carotenoids (some sold as specific 'colour foods') range from dried fruits or flowers, to chemicals such as astazanthin or canthaxanthin (also called Carophyll Red).

CONSEQUENCES

Not only do carotenoids supply colour, they are now known to have health benefits by mopping up toxins called 'free radicals' (these cause ageing and cancer). Vitamin C has this effect too – that is one of the reasons manufacturers add the vitamin in excess of normal requirements.

Research is ongoing in human health to prove the value of carotenoids in our diet – it is expected that these will be equally beneficial to a fish's health. Consequences will be seen in the future!

CHAPTER 8

FEEDING YOUR FISH

The measurement of the actual enjoyment for a given diet is called 'palatability'. Palatability studies show that, like mammals, fish distinguish between taste (gustatory) and smell (olfactory) signals. This so-called gustatory response varies for each species and can even be different for one species from different geographic locations.

It was found that protein and pure amino acids are important chemical attractions for fish. In general, it has been found that herbivorous fish are attracted to some single free amino acids most common to plant protein.

Yellow Tangs (*Zebrasoma flavescens*) are notoriously difficult feeders.

However, carnivorous fish react to a combination of free amino-acids most common to aquatic vertebrate and invertebrate tissues.

For the hobbyist, it means that tempting difficult feeders, such as Yellow Tangs (*Zebrasoma flavescens*), can be achieved with lettuce or peas, but only after the amino-acids are released by blanching (i.e. scalding with very hot water). Tempting carnivores such as a pet Piranha that refuses to eat, is best achieved with chunky pre-cooked shrimp and prawn flesh, rather than with mammalian red meats, or, even worse, feeding live fish which is unnecessary and cruel.

NATURAL FEEDING

The ideal food should be the very diet that the fish eats in its natural home – i.e. live aquatic foods (such as larvae, worms, crustaceans, algae and even smaller fish). The problem is that such foods may carry parasites, bacteria and viruses. Introducing these pathogens to the closed environment of the aquarium will harm the fish.

If you are a breeder and need to feed live foods to stimulate pairing, choose non-aquatic live foods. These can be cultured, such as whiteworms and wingless flies, or garden foods such as red earthworms, green-, white-

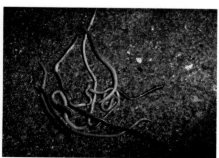

Feeding live foods, such as earthworms, can stimulate breeding.

and black-fly Alternatively, use cultured live foods (e.g. microworms) that have never been exposed to fish pathogens. It is also safe to feed live foods from seawater (such as brine shrimp) to freshwater fish because practically all pathogens of seawater do not affect freshwater animals, and vice versa.

The vitamins, minerals and phytochemicals needed by fish will be present in scrap foods, but not in ideal amounts. That is why a good-quality commercial food needs to be included in all fishes' diets. Where your hobby is just a show tank, the commercial fish food can be fed exclusively for convenience and piece of mind. With a top-quality food, you know that trace elements are being supplied and pollution is kept to a minimum.

Where you own a fish-house and have many mouths to feed, the food bill can be kept down by scrap feeding, but do include at least a weekly feed of a good-quality commercial food.

THE CARNIVORES

Few ornamentals are true carnivores – probably the most famous is the Piranha, *Serrasalmus* species (which is a most unsuitable fish for the home aquarium). Many species need animal protein in their diet, which classifies the fish as a carnivore, but they can exist on cereals and vegetables; this is why early commercial fish foods were nothing more than biscuit meal.

Predatory fish have enzymes that digest whole fish – big fish eat little fish – but many carnivores are 'insectivores' because they feed on, and digest, water- and land-insects. The most famous example is the Archer Fish, *Toxotes jaculatrix,* which spits jets of water at its insect prey (see opposite).

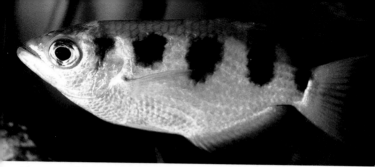

The accomplished insectivore Archer Fish (*Toxotes jaculatrix*) spits out jets of water to hit its target.

What carnivorous fish are looking for in their diets are amino acids already present in the ratios that make up animal or insect flesh. Hence a chunky food made from bird flesh (chicken, turkey, duck and even their eggs) is digested, so too are mammalian meats (beef, mutton, pork, and derived meats such as ham, sausage, corned beef) or offals (liver, kidney, beef heart), that will all be taken with relish.

As shown in the above nutritional information, there is one major problem with this diet, however – the lipids. Mammalian meats contain saturated fats which are harmful to fish. It can even kill them. There are cases where fatty foods (such as portions of a hamburger) have been fed to a pet fish, the fat has solidified in the gut of the fish, and it has then starved to death. In some countries, where BSE is a threat, beef can pose additional problems (though no research has yet been conducted on BSE and fish nutrition).

THE HERBIVORES

The majority of fish species in the wild are the herbivores. They feed on phytoplankton, algae or aquatic plants, and it is on these species that the carnivores prey. The herbivorous fish have long intestines, some with multiple stomachs, to digest the vegetable protein. The goldfish ('the underwater cow') has gut flora that digests cellulose material.

To provide cheap food for humans, fish farming in many tropical countries is based on herbivorous fish converting vegetable matter into fish protein. Grass Carp (*Ctenopharyngodon idella*) are not only fed waste vegetable matter, they are used to control excess aquatic plant growths in canals and ponds. The most popular herbivore in food fish farming are the Tilapia (*Tilapia* and *Oreochromis* species and hybrids) fed on chopped grasses, banana leaves, papaw, rice grains, etc.

No ornamental fish is totally herbivorous, but many need some vegetable protein in their diet. Examples are: Mollies and Guppies, which can be seen to have periods of browsing on the algae growing on the aquarium glass, plastic plants or ornaments, *Leporinus* (American Characins), *Distichodus* (African Characins), *Abramites* (American Headstanders). Other notable examples are Silver Dollars, (e.g. *Metynnis argenteus*) that will quickly devour all the plants in a planted aquarium, as many aquarists have discovered to their cost.

Most ornamental fish need vegetable protein in their diets. Pictured: Cichlids feeding on a lettuce.

The Silver Dollar *Metynnis* sp. is a voracious plant-eater.

THE OMNIVORES

This is by far the largest group of fishes. In fact, many herbivores and even pure carnivores are omnivores at some stage in their growth. This is because fish fry feed on plankton, which includes animal and vegetable (or both) proteinaceous micro-organisms.

The natural foods of wild fish can be categorised as a pyramid, with the plankton and plants at the base, rising through the species (and usually sizes – big fish eat little fish) to the shark at the top.

Another food series is called the 'food web' that shows the range of diets of a given species throughout its life. This can be very complex, involving a web of interrelations of eating and being eaten by aquatic organisms such as bacteria, green plants, molluscs, larvae, crustaceans, and other fishes.

This means that most fishes have an opportunist method of eating, taking in food via sucking, biting, grazing or straining, and via big mouths, tube mouths, scooped mouths, upturned and downturned mouths, and teeth that range from needles to plate grinders. They take in organic matter by whatever method evolution has developed, and digest their needs, excreting the remainder. This is why most fish are true omnivores – they can eat anything.

CHAPTER
9

FOOD FORMULATIONS

Nothing can compare with a good-quality commercial dry feed. Available in flake, granule, pellet, tablet, stick and powdered forms, the dried food supplies all the nutrients that pet fish require, but minus the water (which is not needed of course).

The advantage of drying is that the shelf life can be very long indeed and the food is not subject to spoilage by bacteria or fungus. Flake forms are particularly useful. They sink for bottom-feeders, but only slowly, so mid-water feeders can take the flakes, and they will float (if placed flat on the surface) for the top-feeders. The smallest fry can nibble food from a large flake and even large fish can 'hoover' up small flakes.

◀ Good-quality flake food is nutritious, and suitable for a large range of species.

Food sticks can be fed ▶ occasionally if your fish require a temporary change of diet.

SHELF LIFE

The drying process only removes water, which is not required in the food by fish, but this imparts a long shelf life for the flake food. At 4 per cent moisture levels, or less, the foodstuff cannot support bacteria or allow fungus to grow. To retain this low moisture level, the flake must be packed in a sealed pot and an inert atmosphere, which is only done with good-quality foods. Expect to pay a premium for a good-quality food packed in expensive but effective packaging. Cheap food means poor nutrition.

However, once opened, all fish food deteriorates, especially in the moist atmosphere of a fish-house, or if left on top of the aquarium (where it gets hot).

Always reseal (where possible) the pot of dried foods. Even then, the vitamin content (especially the important vitamin C) will fade in a matter of weeks, so buy dried foods in small pots that will get used within three months.

Pellets, sticks, and granules are less versatile and often lower in nutritional value, mainly because they are expanded (i.e. blown up with air).

Tablet food is compressed flaked food. It is a useful form of food to leave with a fish minder if you are going away for a long time as it is easier to dose correctly (e.g. two tablets per day or whatever). Tablets

Tablet food, attached to the glass, is a useful means of exhibiting fish.

can also be useful for exclusive feeding of bottom-dwellers, or targeting night-feeders.

Some tablets will stick to the front glass, which will bring the fish forward for group feeding – useful for showing off the tank contents to visitors.

THE BABIES

Commercial foods for fry are standard flake or granules ground to a pepper-like powder. It may be coarse for the large fry of livebearers or very fine for the tiny baby fish from some egglayers, or made into a paste or liquid with preservatives added.

For better nutrition, a protein booster is usually added to help growth. One such booster is fish protein concentrate (FPC), a commercial powder made from ground seafish deemed unsuitable for marketing as wet fish. Sometimes powdered egg is added to the food, since this is a very good protein source in terms of balanced amino-acids.

Home-made baby fish foods can be made from red earthworms and a little water, macerated in a kitchen blender (perhaps not the actual kitchen model!). Pour the purée into a dish and allow the soil to sink and the shredded worm to float, which can be scooped off for frequent feeds to the fry. The protein content is ideal.

Freshly-hatched brine shrimp remains the best growth food for baby fish after a week or so, but always use a commercial flake or commercial fry food, to ensure that essential trace elements are given.

SCRAP FOODS

Basically, if you can eat it, they can eat it! Hence, anything you have in the larder is potential fish food,

Scrap foods should be fed with care. White and oily fish are ideal and small quantities of meat are acceptable if the fat is trimmed off. Dairy products should never be fed, however.

which cuts the feeding bill if you have dozens of tanks in a fish-house. However, in view of the nutritional information shown above, there are certain foods which should be avoided.

FATTY FOODS

The information on lipids (page 16) shows that any foods containing hard fat (e.g. burgers, corned beef, etc.) must not be fed to fish. Dairy products should be avoided too, since they contain milk fats, or cereal products that are blended with dairy fats (e.g. most biscuits).

MEATS

Feed sparingly with the various meats – raw beef, lamb, pork or venison etc. They can be used for carnivores and to tempt difficult feeders, but not on a regular basis or damage could be caused to the fishes' livers.

Cooked meats are acceptable and may have lower fat content. Low-fat meats (chicken, turkey and game) are better than mammalian meats. Again, they can be shredded raw or cooked.

OFFALS

'Offals' are a good source of rich foods to tempt difficult fish or to condition for breeding. Beef heart has been used for many years, especially by the Discus breeders, so too has raw liver and kidney. These are acceptable if fed sparingly and provided the fat is trimmed off, especially if prepared in bulk for freezing to store. But again, meats and offal should not be the main diet – in the wild, fish will never encounter such foods.

NATURAL CHOICE

The foodstuffs that fish do find in the wild, that is available as a scrap diet, are fish meats and shellfish. White fish, oily fish, shrimps, prawns, crabs, mussels, are an excellent choice. They can be cooked or raw but take care not to overfeed as messy foods can easily pollute the water.

WET FOODS

Some aquarium shops have freezer units and so can offer a range of fish foods that are preserved by freezing. Unfortunately, freezing does not destroy all the bacteria (but it will destroy all parasites) so some manufacturers give the frozen food a small dose of

Gamma-irradiated frozen food provides a safe alternative to live food. Pictured: blood worms, glassworms, brine shrimps and *Daphnia* sold in blister packs.

gamma radiation to sterilize it. This type of food is particularly useful for supplying 'safe' natural foods, such as *Tubifex*, bloodworms, and *Daphnia* etc., needed to bring breeding pairs into condition.

Keep such foods in the freezer (separately wrapped from domestic foods) and always just cut or snap off enough for a day or two's feeding. Never allow the bulk to thaw and then refreeze it, or the sterilization effected by the radiation will be lost and the food will deteriorate, even in the freezer.

Freeze-dried forms of these natural foods are also available as a treat and can be safely used and stored like dried foods.

LIVE FOODS

Feeding live aquatic foods to your fish from a wild source is not recommended – they carry bacteria, viruses and often parasites that will affect your fish. Live aquatic foods include *Tubifex*, *Daphnia*, Cyclops and Mosquito Larvae.

Elephant fish enjoying a bloodworm meal.

If you want to feed these as a treat, as a stimulus for breeding, or to colour for showing, use the freeze-dried or frozen forms, which kill off most of the pathogens.

It is better to choose a non-aquatic live food, where parasites, bacteria and viruses do exist but the aquatic environment is alien to them and so they are not infectious. Garden earthworms are an excellent example, or the cultured worms: white and grindal. More details on the culture of live foods can be found in another title in this *Practical Fishkeeping* series (*Live Foods for Aquarium Fishes*, by John Rundle).

One wild source of live foods that is safe are flies (green, white or black) from garden flowers but not if the garden is sprayed with any chemicals, of course.

Use a paintbrush to remove greenfly from roses so that you can feed them to your fish.

CONSEQUENCES

- For a simple, reliable and safe diet, feed your pet fish on a good-quality commercial dried food.
- For a treat, use irradiated, frozen natural foods.
- To save money and bring a little variety, try shredded samples of your own meals but avoid anything fatty.
- To bring the fish into breeding condition, use live foods, but these must be clean or safe, i.e. cultured or gathered from a non-aquatic environment.

Little and often is the best way, but, if you lead a busy life, once-a-day feeding in the evening is acceptable. It is better to divide that food into two lots, fed morning and evening. If you have the time, divide into three and feed the fish when you have your own meals three times a day.

Quantity depends on species and stocking levels. The best advice is 'as much as can be consumed in two or three minutes'. Remove any surplus thereafter – with daily feeding, you will soon learn how much is taken in those few minutes and so feed just enough.

GOING AWAY

If you go away, the fish can be safely left without food for a week, even a fortnight if they are adult and the aquarium is mature. This is because the water is full of micro-organisms and algae that will keep the fish going until you return.

If the fish are fry or the tank is brand new, allow a friend to feed (and check the system) daily or at least weekly. However, beware of leaving a pot full of fish food. Innocent fish minders will respond to 'begging' for food by adding too much and polluting the water. Weigh out a single portion for the day or week.

Fish are unlikely to die of starvation in mature waters but they certainly will die from overfeeding.

CHAPTER 10

NUTRITIONAL RESEARCH

The 20th century saw a dramatic increase in the knowledge of companion animal nutrition and its role in health. Dog, cat and pet bird nutrition have been studied, and the results used to prepare the ideal pet foods in a fiercely competitive market.

Research into fish nutrition has taken a different route – it is mainly concerned with fish farming and the requirement for fast growth for the edible fish market. The studies are generally for Masters and Doctorate degrees or are funded by governments with the aim of providing cheap protein sources for the populations of emerging countries. Hence most published data on fish nutrition covers the needs of edible fishes such as tilapia, carp and catfish, but not ornamentals.

ORNAMENTAL FISH

Fish food manufacturers use these values for the nutritional requirements of ornamental fishes. Although better than nothing, it is not good science to interpret the needs of one species as valid for another. Hence some international companies have funded research into the specific nutritional needs of the most popular ornamental fishes. The reason for these quite expensive projects is to improve their commercial brands of fish food and so succeed in a very competitive world market – with obvious advantages for aquarists and their fish.

A technician is watching an automatic feeder dispensing pre-weighed quantities of flake food.

THE FUTURE OF RESEARCH

Waltham®, a leading authority on pet care and nutrition, studies the needs of ornamental fishes. Its research unit (the Waltham® Aquacentre) contains special aquaria where known quantities of food are offered to baby fish and where they are weighed daily as they grow. Their excreta is swept from the aquaria by a water flow system that concentrates the faeces in a settling tube.

The faeces are collected and pressed into a tablet form that is burnt in a calorimeter to give the calorific value of undigested food. This can be compared with the known calorific values of the recipes fed to the fish and so calculations made for the DE, ME and GE (see chapter 4) values per rates of growth.

Fish faeces being collected from the settling tube for weighing and measuring calorific values.

A goldfish, making the choice of two foods on a frame.

Preferences for a particular recipe are measured by offering the fish two choices on a special frame and the number of 'hits' recorded by technicians observing the reactions of the fish.

This kind of research has been carried out for more than 25 years and a great deal of valuable data has been collected, with the results published in various scientific journals.

Waltham® Aquacentre research and data has also been used in this book, which I hope has been interesting, informative and of practical use in our most fascinating of all hobbies – ornamental fishkeeping.